A Guide for Using

Because of Winn-Dixie

in the Classroom

Based on the novel written by Kate DiCamillo

*This guide written by **Melissa Hart***

Teacher Created Materials, Inc.
6421 Industry Way
Westminster, CA 92683
www.teachercreated.com
©2003 Teacher Created Materials
Reprinted, 2003
Made in U.S.A.
ISBN 0-7439-3159-9

Edited by
Stephanie Buehler, Psy.D.

Illustrated by
Sue Fullam

Cover Art by
Kevin Barnes

Table of Contents

- Quiz Time
- Hands-on Project: Dog Decoupage and Facts
- Cooperative Learning Activity: Group Story
- Curriculum Connections: *Life Skills*—Grocery Store Adventures
- Into Your Life: Description

- Quiz Time
- Hands-on Project: Your Own Storybook
- Cooperative Learning Activity: Library Adventure
- Curriculum Connections: *Geography*—All About Florida
- Into Your Life: Understanding Prejudice

- Quiz Time
- Hands-on Project: Bottle Tree
- Cooperative Learning Activity: Similes and Metaphors
- Curriculum Connections: *History*—The Civil War
- Into Your Life: Understanding Disabilities

- Quiz Time
- Hands-on Project: Making Candy
- Cooperative Learning Activity: Community Volunteering
- Curriculum Connections: *Science/Math*—Thunderstorm!
- Into Your Life: Life Is Like a Littmus Lozenge

- Quiz Time
- Hands-on Project: Luminarias
- Cooperative Learning Activity: Classmate Interviews
- Curriculum Connections: *Cooking*—Egg Salad and Dump Punch
- Into Your Life: Making Friends

After the Book (Post-reading Activities)

Introduction

A good book can enrich lives like a good friend. Fictional characters can inspire us and teach us about the world in which we live. We can turn to books for companionship, entertainment, and guidance. A truly beloved book may touch our lives forever. Great care has been taken with Literature Units to select books that are sure to become your students' good friends.

Teachers who use this unit will find the following features to supplement their own ideas:

- Sample lesson plans

- Pre-reading activities

- A biographical sketch and picture of the author

- A book summary

- Vocabulary lists and suggested vocabulary activities

- Chapters are grouped for study. Each section includes the following:

  —quiz

  —hands-on project

  —cooperative learning activity

  —cross-curricular connection

  —extension into the reader's life

- Post-reading activities

- Book report ideas

- Research activities

- Culminating activities

- Three different options for unit tests

- Bibliography of related reading

- Answer key

The hope is that this unit will be a valuable addition to your own curriculum ideas to supplement *Because of Winn-Dixie*.

Sample Lesson Plan

The time it takes to complete the suggested lessons below will vary, depending on the type of activity, your students' abilities, and interest levels.

Lesson 1
- Introduce and complete some or all of the pre-reading activities from "Before Reading the Book." (page 5)
- Read "About the Author" with students. (page 6)
- Introduce the vocabulary list for Section 1. (page 8)

Lesson 2
- Read Chapters 1–5. As you read, discuss vocabulary words, using the book context to discern their meanings.
- Locate Gainesville, Florida on a classroom map. Author Kate DiCamillo graduated from college in Gainesville.
- Choose a vocabulary activity to complete. (page 9)
- Complete "Dog Decoupage and Facts." (page 11)
- Write a "Group Story." (page 12)
- Go on a "Grocery Store Adventure." (page 13)
- Observe your surroundings. (page 14)
- Administer the Section 1 Quiz. (page 10)
- Introduce the vocabulary list for Section 2. (page 8)

Lesson 3
- Read Chapters 6–10. Discuss vocabulary words.
- Choose a vocabulary activity to complete. (page 9)
- Complete "Your Own Storybook." (page 16)
- Go on a "Library Adventure." (page 17)
- Learn about Florida. (page 18)
- Discuss "Understanding Prejudice." (page 19)
- Administer the Section 2 Quiz. (page 15)
- Introduce the vocabulary list for Section 3. (page 8)

Lesson 4
- Read Chapters 11–15. Discuss vocabulary words.
- Choose a vocabulary activity to complete. (page 9)
- Make a bottle tree. (page 21)
- Create similes and metaphors. (page 22)

- Research and discuss the Civil War. (page 23)
- Complete "Understanding Disabilities." (page 24)
- Administer the Section 3 Quiz. (page 20)
- Introduce the vocabulary list for Section 4. (page 8)

Lesson 5
- Read Chapters 16–20. Discuss vocabulary words.
- Choose a vocabulary activity to complete. (page 9)
- Explore "Community Volunteering." (page 27)
- Learn about thunderstorms. (page 28)
- Complete "Life is Like a Litmus Lozenge." (page 29)
- Administer the Section 4 Quiz. (page 25)
- Introduce the vocabulary list for Section 5. (page 8)

Lesson 6
- Read Chapters 21–26. Discuss vocabulary words.
- Choose a vocabulary activity to complete. (page 9)
- Make luminarias. (page 31)
- Complete "Classmate Interviews." (page 32)
- Make egg salad sandwiches and Dump Punch. (page 33)
- Discuss friendship. (page 34)
- Administer the Section 5 Quiz. (page 30)

Lesson 7
- Discuss questions students have about the book. (page 35)
- Assign a book report and research activity. (pages 36–37)
- Begin work on one or more culminating activities. (pages 38–42)

Lesson 8
- Choose and administer one or more of the Unit Tests. (pages 43–45)
- Discuss students' feelings about the book.
- Provide a bibliography of related reading. (page 46)

Before Reading the Book

Before you begin reading *Because of Winn-Dixie* with your students, complete one or more of the following pre-reading activities to stimulate their interest and enhance their comprehension.

1. Examine the cover of the book. Ask students to predict the book's plot, characters, and setting.

2. Discuss the title. Ask students who or what they think Winn-Dixie is, and see if they can predict anything about the book from its title.

3. Answer these questions:

   • Why might a 10-year-old girl have no mother?

   • What would it be like to move to a new town and not yet have made any new friends?

   ✓ • What would you do if you found a stray dog?

   ✓ • Can a young person be a friend to a much older person?

   ✓ • What do you know about Florida?

   • What might it be like to be the child of a preacher?

   • What are your feelings about people with disabilities such as blindness or mental retardation?

   • Can life be both good and bad at the same time?

4. Direct students to work in groups to brainstorm what a new child in town might do in order to make friends. Share your suggestions with the class.

5. Direct students to work in groups to list the different disabilities or illnesses that students are aware of. This novel includes characters with alcoholism, mental retardation, and blindness. Discuss the challenges that physically and mentally handicapped people must overcome.

6. Brainstorm the different gifts an older person might bring to a friendship with a younger person. Then, brainstorm the gifts a young person might bring to a friendship with an older person. (Encourage students to think of gifts in terms of intangibles. For instance, an older person may give the gifts of wisdom and teaching. A younger person may give the gifts of time and interest.)

7. Work in groups to discuss how animals help humans. Students may make a list of their own pets and how these pets have helped them.

About the Author

Kate DiCamillo was born in Philadelphia, Pennsylvania. She had a difficult childhood. When she was five years old, her father left her family. She also suffered from chronic pneumonia. A doctor advised her mother to move Kate to a warmer climate, where her symptoms might be helped. Later that year, Kate found herself living in Florida.

She loved growing up in Florida because people were friendly. Everyone in her small town knew one another. They talked slowly and said words like *ain't* and *y'all*. Some of the characters in *Because of Winn-Dixie* speak in this same Florida dialect that Kate loved so much as a child.

Kate earned her bachelor's degree in English from the University of Florida. She moved to Minnesota in her twenties. As a child, Kate had always wanted to write and tell stories. Some of her favorite childhood books were *The Yearling, Ribsy*, and *The Secret Garden*. She started writing children's books after she got a job on the children's floor in a bookstore. In her early days of writing, she set her alarm for 4:00 A.M. so that she could write before taking off to work at a used book store.

Kate writes for both children and adults. She wrote *Because of Winn-Dixie* during a harsh winter in Minnesota. She missed Florida and the people. Suddenly, she had the idea for a character named India Opal Buloni and her dog.

The book appeared on the *New York Times* bestseller list and won awards, among them the prestigious Newbery Honor award. After she received the phone call from the Newbery committee, Kate was so surprised that she accidentally walked into walls all day!

Kate currently lives in Minneapolis, Minnesota. She still writes two pages a day, five days a week, no matter how busy she is. She has worked with a critique group of writers for five years. They read each other's writing aloud every other week and comment on it.

You can find out more about Kate DiCamillo on her publisher's website at *www.candlewick.com*. There, she talks about her passion for writing, saying: "E. B. White said, 'All that I hope to say in books, all that I ever hope to say, is that I love the world.'" Kate adds, "That's the way I feel, too."

Because of Winn-Dixie

by Kate DiCamillo

(Candlewick, 2000)

Because of Winn-Dixie begins when 10-year old India Opal Buloni moves to Naomi, Florida, with her preacher father. She has no friends, and she is still grieving the loss of her mother, who left when she was three years old. The children at her church appear unfriendly or too young with whom to be friends. Her father works constantly and doesn't want to talk very much. Opal is lonely.

Life begins to look up for Opal when she finds a stray dog in a grocery store. The manager is about to call the pound when Opal steps in to rescue the dog. She names him Winn-Dixie, after the supermarket in which he was found. Winn-Dixie turns out to be an extraordinary dog. He has all sorts of quirks that make people laugh. His personality endears him to Opal, her father, and the rest of the community. Thanks in part to her dog, Opal gradually begins to develop friendships in the most unexpected places, including the library and a pet store. She gets a job in the pet store, and she discovers something mysterious about the man who works there with her.

Throughout the story, Opal struggles with issues of prejudice. She challenges two boys when they call one of her friends a witch. She also overcomes her own prejudices, thanks to good advice from an older woman. Opal discovers that people aren't always what they appear to be, and she learns what it means to be a good friend. When she stops thinking only about herself and gives time, care, and attention to others, she finds happiness.

Near the end of the story, Opal brings all of her friends together for a party. She reflects on her newfound joy. However, this happiness is almost destroyed when she loses the very dearest friend of all. During this difficult time, she learns to understand her father better.

Because of Winn-Dixie ends with a vivid reminder of the power of friendship, which can help us through both the sweet and bitter moments of life.

Vocabulary Lists

Below are lists of vocabulary words and idiomatic phrases for each section of chapters. The following page offers ideas for using this vocabulary in classroom activities.

Section 1: Chapters 1–5

skidded	produce (*n.*)	missionary	distract(ed)	sermon
suffering	exception	fortunate (*n.*)	effect	constellations
judge (*v.*)	memorized	congregation	potluck	retriever

Section 2: Chapters 6–10

memorial	embarrassed	trembling	snuffle(d)	palmetto
pride(ful)	peculiar	recall(s)	grand	advanced (*adj.*)
gerbil	installment (plan)	dust bunnies	trustworthy	theme
overgrown	green thumb			

Section 3: Chapters 11–15

whimper(ing)	tearing (*v.*)	pathological	intend	criminal
charming (*v.*)	routine	cooped up	retarded	
roundabout	fit (*n.*)	rights	dramatic	

Section 4: Chapters 16–20

occur(red)	enlist(ed)	abiding	typhoid	survive(d)
sensation	lozenge	sorrow	manufacture(d)	hunch(ing)
melancholy	batch	tragedies	squawk(ed)	murderer

Section 5: Chapters 21–26

frilly	crepe paper	shimmer(y)	gentle	complicated
downpour	drizzle	plumb (*slang*)	spells	potions
myths	strum(med)			

8

Vocabulary Activities

You can help your students learn the vocabulary words in *Because of Winn-Dixie* by providing them with the stimulating vocabulary activities below.

- Ask students to work in groups to create an illustrated book of the vocabulary words and their meanings.

- Group students. Direct groups to use vocabulary words to create crossword puzzles and word searches. Groups can trade puzzles to complete and then check each other's work.

- In small groups, play "Guess the Definition." One student writes down the correct definition of the vocabulary word. The others write down false definitions, close enough to the original definition that their classmates might be fooled. Read all definitions, and then challenge students to guess the correct one. Students whose definitions mislead their classmates get a point for each student fooled.

- Use a vocabulary word in five different sentences. Compare sentences and discuss.

- Write a short story using as many of the words as possible. Students may then read their stories in groups.

- Encourage students to use each new vocabulary word in a conversation five times during a single day. They can take notes on how and when the word was used, and then share their experience with the class.

- Play "Vocabulary Charades." Each student or group of students gets a word to act out. Other students must guess the word.

- Play "Vocabulary Pictures." Each student or group of students must draw a picture representing a word on the chalkboard or on paper. Other students must guess the word.

- Challenge students to a "Vocabulary Bee." In small groups or independently, students must spell each word correctly and give its proper definition.

- Talk about the different forms that a word may take. For instance, some words may function as both nouns and verbs. The word *judge* is a good example of a word which can be both a noun and a verb. Some words look alike but may have completely different meanings. In *Because of Winn-Dixie*, the word *tearing* is used to describe a dog racing around, but it may also be used to describe the act of ripping or eyes watering.

- Ask students to make flash cards by writing a vocabulary word on one side of an index card and its definition on the other. Ask them to work with a younger class to help them learn the definitions of the new words, using the flash cards.

- Write vocabulary words on stiff paper with glue, and then cover the glue with glitter or sand. Alternatively, students may write the words with a squeeze bottle full of jam on bread to create an edible lesson!

Quiz Time

Answer the following questions about Chapters 1–5.

1. How does Opal rescue Winn-Dixie in the first chapter?_____

   _____

2. What characteristics does Opal like about Winn-Dixie?_____

   _____

3. How does Opal feel about her father? Why? _____

   _____

4. Why does Opal's father agree to let her keep Winn-Dixie? _____

   _____

5. What does Opal do to Winn-Dixie to try to improve his appearance?_____

   _____

6. Why do you think Opal's mother left her and the preacher? _____

   _____

7. Why does the preacher allow Winn-Dixie to go to church?_____

   _____

8. What does Opal pray for in church at the end of Chapter 5? _____

   _____

Dog Decoupage and Facts

The word *decoupage* comes from the French word *découper*, which means *to cut up*. In art, decoupage refers to the technique of decorating items with cut-up pieces of paper, then glazing them with lacquer to create a beautiful ornament. Many things can be transformed using decoupage—empty milk cartons, shoeboxes, empty frozen orange juice containers, and even flowerpots.

Materials

- old magazines, catalogs, and newspapers
- empty frozen orange juice cylinders, small boxes, milk cartons, flowerpots, or other small items to decorate

- scissors
- glue
- flat 2" paintbrush

Directions

Choose an item to decoupage. From magazines, catalogs, and newspapers, cut out pictures and words that relate to dogs. Glue these onto your item, overlapping them slightly to completely cover the surface. Let your decoupage dry for a day, and then brush white glue over the surface as a lacquer. Let your new art piece dry once more.

Dog Facts

Use encyclopedias, books, the Internet, and experts such as breeders to find out interesting facts about dogs. Then complete the form below.

1. What reference materials or resources did you use to research facts about dogs?

   _____

2. List the three most interesting things that you learned about dogs during your research.

   a. _____

   b. _____

   c. _____

3. List one fact about dogs that surprised you. Write a different fact than those already listed.

   _____

   _____

4. If you could own any dog, what type of dog would it be? What would you name him or her?

   _____

Group Story

Opal's father tells her that her mother loved a good story. Later on in *Because of Winn-Dixie*, Opal learns to love stories herself. People have been telling stories for thousands of years. Before books, humans used stories, songs, and poems to pass down history, morals, and other important information to later generations. This practice is called the "oral tradition."

Materials

- three stapled sheets of lined paper per student

- pens or pencils

- watch or clock with a second hand

Teacher Preparation

Write the following story introductions on the board.

1. One day, a girl named Susie found a five-dollar bill on the sidewalk.

2. Marvin and Melvyn were twins, but they always argued.

3. During a bad thunderstorm, Carlos got lost in the woods near his house and saw a mountain lion.

4. Katie, always scared of bugs, screamed as the spider crawled up her arm.

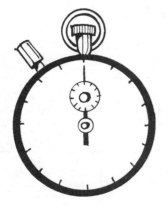

Directions

Distribute writing materials. Tell students that they have 30 seconds to write their favorite story introduction at the top of the first sheet of paper in their packet. Let them know that you are the timekeeper, and that as soon as you call time, students are to pass their packets to the left. Students then have 30 seconds or so to add to the story, then pass their papers to the left again. Group stories can continue as long as time and interest allow. You may allow slightly more time as the stories progress, giving students time to read the previous parts of the story before adding to them. At the end of the exercise, students can share the final stories.

Grocery Store Adventure

Opal finds Winn-Dixie in a grocery store in Naomi, Florida. The dog knocks tomatoes, onions, and green peppers all over the floor. Dogs do not belong in grocery stores, but people do. People have been going to grocery stores and markets for centuries in order to buy food and other needed items. This activity, which gives students practice with grocery shopping, may be completed as a field trip or as homework.

Materials

- pen or pencil for each group
- copy of the form below for each group

Directions

Separate students into groups of three. Explain that you will be taking a field trip to the local grocery store. Each student is to pretend to have one dollar to spend on groceries. Students will be working in small groups to fill out the form below. To culminate the activity, lead a discussion in which students compare their findings about what they can and cannot purchase with a dollar.

Grocery Store Questions

1. Write the cost per pound of bananas. How many bananas can you buy for a dollar?_____

   _____

2. Write the cost of the most expensive loaf of bread you can find. Write down the cost of the least expensive loaf. Can you buy a loaf of bread for a dollar?_____

   _____

3. Write the cost per pound of brown onions. How many brown onions can you buy for a dollar?

   _____

4. Write the cost of the most expensive and least expensive cans of dog food you can find. Which food would your group feed a dog, and why?_____

   _____

5. If Opal had a dollar, what kind of a toy could she afford to buy Winn-Dixie in this grocery store?

   _____

6. Write the cost of a carton of eggs (choose a brand). How much would a single egg cost?

   _____

7. List ten items in the grocery store that cost about one dollar each. _____

   _____

   _____

   _____

Into Your Life: Description

Opal describes the Open Arms Baptist Church of Naomi, Florida, in great detail. She notes that it used to be a Pick-It-Quick store, and that the store's name is still spelled out in red tiles at the front of the building. She also describes that, instead of traditional church pews, people bring their own folding chairs to sit on during the sermon. These descriptions of place are called *setting*. Setting is an important component of both life and literature. It refers to place, as well as to time and season.

Practice recording the elements of your own current setting by describing your classroom in a paragraph. Be as detailed as possible.

_____

_____

_____

_____

_____

Now, describe your favorite place in one paragraph. It may be indoors or outdoors. Write down as many details as possible to show what makes this place original and interesting.

_____

_____

_____

_____

_____

Share your description with classmates.

Quiz Time

Answer the following questions about Chapters 6-10.

1. Why does Miss Franny Block finally allow Winn-Dixie into the library? _____

   _____

2. How did Miss Franny obtain the Herman W. Block Memorial Library? _____

   _____

3. What does Opal promise to do so that she can earn Winn-Dixie a red collar and leash from the pet
   store? _____

   _____

4. Why is Opal so happy at the end of Chapter 8? _____

   _____

5. Why doesn't Opal like Stevie and Dunlap Dewberry? _____

   _____

6. How does Opal finally end up going into Gloria Dump's yard? _____

   _____

7. How has Winn-Dixie helped Opal make new friends? _____

   _____

8. What amazes Opal at the end of Chapter 10? _____

   _____

Your Own Storybook

Stories are important in *Because of Winn-Dixie*. Many people tell them, including Opal's father, Miss Franny Block, Gloria Dump, and Otis.

Stories include several parts. Here are a few of the most important ones:

Characters: These are the people in your story. For instance, characters in *Because of Winn-Dixie* include Opal, her dog, her father, Gloria Dump, Otis, and others. Each character has a challenge to overcome.

Setting: This is where and when your story takes place. Opal's story takes place in Florida in summertime, before school has started and she has had the chance to make friends.

Plot: This is what happens in your story. For instance, Opal is very lonely at the beginning of the book. Then she finds a dog and makes new friends, but it is only when something terrifying happens that she learns how important relationships are.

Dialogue: These are words spoken by characters. Many of the characters in *Because of Winn-Dixie* speak in a Southern dialect, which is a certain way of saying things.

Materials

- lined paper for rough drafts
- 2 sheets of 8 ½" x 11" (22 cm x 28 cm) cardboard-backed, vinyl-covered paper
- 12 sheets of white 8 ½" x 11" (22 cm x 28 cm) paper
- yarn
- hole punch

Directions

1. Organize a chart of the characters, setting, and plot of a story you would like to write. Write the rough draft on lined paper, making sure to include dialogue between the characters.

2. Now, punch two holes in the vinyl-covered front cover-sheet, ½" (1.3 cm) from the left edge and 2" (5 cm) down from the top and bottom edges. Use this cover sheet as a stencil to mark the location of the holes on the white center sheets and the back cover. Punch holes in the center sheets and back cover. Thread yarn in and out of the holes a few times so that your bookbinding is strong. Tie a bow on the front cover.

3. Write the final draft of your story in your book. Illustrate it and share it with your class.

Library Adventure

Opal spends much of her summer in the Herman W. Block Memorial Library, where Miss Franny Block tells her wonderful stories about the past. Libraries began in the Middle East between 3000 and 2000 B.C. Today, nearly every town and school has a library full of exciting books, magazines, and much more.

Students may complete the following activity at either the school or local library. Contact the librarian beforehand to let him or her know that a class is coming to do research. Ask the librarian to provide students with a brief tour of the library so that they know where to look for the needed information.

Materials

- one copy of "Library Questions" for each group of three students

- pencils

Directions

After touring the library, divide the class into groups of three. Each group should have a copy of the questions below. Stagger the library starting points and corresponding questions among the groups so that they are all not trying to look at the same resource at the same time.

Library Questions

1. You would like to read *Because of Winn-Dixie* again, but you don't have a copy. Where do you go in the library to find this novel? How is this section of the library organized? _____

   _____

2. You'd like to find out more about Kate DiCamillo, the author of *Because of Winn-Dixie*. Go to a computer and type her name into an Internet search engine such as one of the following:

        • *www.google.com*   • *www.yahoo.com*   • *www.netscape.com*

   Write down the name of one Web site that contains information about Kate DiCamillo.

   _____

3. Stories about *Because of Winn-Dixie* and Kate DiCamillo have appeared in several magazines. Where do you go in the library to research magazine articles? Write down the name of one magazine in which an article related to *Because of Winn-Dixie* or the author appears.

   _____

4. In reading this novel, you become interested in Florida. Use an encyclopedia to find an article about this state. Write down the page numbers of the article. Then write down one interesting fact you read about Florida. _____

   _____

5. Now that you are reading *Because of Winn-Dixie*, you are interested in dogs. Where do you go in the library to find factual information about dogs? Write down the title, as well as the call number (the number on the spine of the book jacket) of one book that you found on this subject.

All About Florida

Directions: Use reference books and/or the Internet to find these facts about Florida.

Area: _____   State Nickname: _____

Capital City: _____   Time Zone: _____

State Flower: _____   Climate: _____

State Motto: _____   National Park(s): _____

Find the city of Gainesville on a map of Florida. Kate DiCamillo, the author of *Because of Winn-Dixie*, graduated from the University of Florida in Gainesville.

1. Label the ocean that is closest to Gainsville.

2. Find the three largest cities in Florida and label them on the map.

3. What is a peninsula? _____

   _____

4. What country is directly south of Florida?

   _____

5. What country is southwest?

   _____

Understanding Prejudice

The word *prejudice* refers to the concept of forming an opinion about someone before really knowing him or her. There are many instances of prejudice in *Because of Winn-Dixie*. Stevie and Dunlap show prejudice toward Gloria Dump when they call her a witch. Opal shows prejudice toward Amanda Wilkinson when she calls her "pinch-faced" before really getting to know her.

Many people have some form of prejudice toward people they don't know. But prejudice can be dangerous. It can lead to hurtful speech and even hate crimes. Gloria Dump tells Opal, "You can't always judge people by the things they done. You got to judge them by what they are doing now." This is one good way to overcome prejudice.

Activities

1. Break into groups. Using newspapers and/or magazines, find one example of prejudice. Answer the following questions:

   What type of prejudice is being described? _____

   Who showed this prejudice? _____

   What happened as a result of this prejudice? _____

   What advice would you give this person to overcome his/her prejudice? _____

   _____

2. Discuss with the class how name-calling makes a person feel. Talk about courteous ways to behave around a person with a physical or developmental disability (for example, not staring or pointing, but treating the person with respect). Ask students to list some ways to overcome prejudice, such as finding out more about people as individuals or seeking information about different groups of people to increase understanding.

3. Discuss the idea of stereotypes with students, which is the human tendency to see all people with some characteristic in the same way. Different stereotypes include ageism, physical beauty, clothing styles, etc. Then break students into groups. Using newspapers and/or magazines, have each group find one example of stereotyping and then complete a chart such as the one below.

What type of stereotype or prejudice did you find?	
How is the stereotype described?	
Who is showing prejudice against this stereotype?	
What happened as a result of this prejudice?	

Quiz Time

Answer the following questions about Chapters 11–15.

1. Why does Opal's father say that Winn-Dixie has a pathological fear of thunderstorms? _____

   _____

2. What is Opal feeling at the end of Chapter 11? Why? _____

   _____

3. Why does Otis play music for the animals in the pet shop?_____

   _____

4. Describe Opal's and Winn-Dixie's daily routine that summer._____

   _____

5. Why does Opal get mad at Stevie? _____

   _____

6. Why does Gloria Dump have a bottle tree in her yard? _____

   _____

7. What does Gloria Dump tell Opal about judging people? _____

   _____

8. Name two reasons that Opal holds tightly onto Winn-Dixie that summer. _____

   _____

Bottle Tree

Gloria Dump surprises Opal by showing her a bottle tree. Gloria's tree is full of whiskey and beer bottles—"the ghosts of all the things I done wrong," she says. You and your classmates can make a bottle tree symbolizing all the things your class has done right.

Materials

- lined paper, one sheet per student

- a schoolyard tree, potted tree, or sturdy branch

- yarn

- scissors

- small plastic bottles with labels removed

Directions

Ask students to bring a small plastic bottle from home. Then ask each student to write down one good thing he or she has accomplished this year on a piece of paper. You may or may not ask students to stand up in class and share these good deeds. Students then roll up their papers and place them inside their bottles. Assist them in tying the bottles onto the tree or branch with lengths of yarn.

Discuss the reasons why Gloria Dump created her bottle tree. Do students feel that this is a good way to remember the bad things that someone once did so that they won't repeat them? How does the class feel about its more positive bottle tree? You may choose to leave an indoor tree or branch in one corner of the classroom as a reminder of the students' accomplishments.

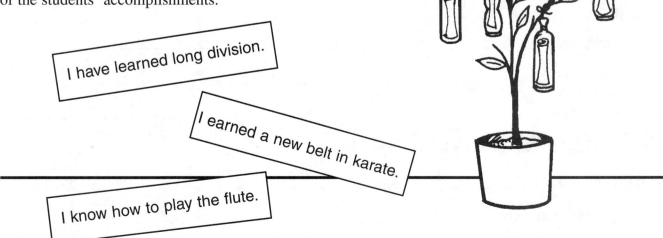

I have learned long division.

I earned a new belt in karate.

I know how to play the flute.

Similes and Metaphors

Figurative language refers to language that compares one thing with another in order to make it come alive for the reader. This type of language includes similes and metaphors.

A simile compares one thing to another using the words *like* or *as*. For instance, Opal said, *"Winn-Dixie* looked like a furry bullet" when her dog ran after the mouse in church. She compares the dog to a bullet in order to help the reader see the action more precisely.

A metaphor compares two things without using the words *like* or *as*. Opal says about her father, "I could see him pulling his old turtle head back into his stupid turtle shell." Opal is comparing her still-grieving father to a turtle hiding.

Activity: Break into groups of four. Using the form below create similes and four metaphors to share with your classmates.

Similes

- Getting to play in the schoolyard at recess is like _____

- Being ill with the flu is like _____

- Finding a dollar bill is as _____

- Forgetting your lunch or your lunch money is as_____

- Eating noodles is like eating _____

- A cat's fur is like_____

- Riding a horse is like_____

Metaphors

- Summer vacation is_____

- Breaking a favorite toy or game is _____

- Eating ice cream on a hot summer day is_____

- Sitting in class when you really want to be home is _____

- The full moon is _____

- The fog coming in over the hill is_____

- The dry creek is_____

The Civil War

In Chapter 15, Miss Franny Block tells Opal about the Civil War. This was a war between the United States and the Confederate States. It lasted from 1861 to 1865. The immediate cause of the war was slavery. The Southern states allowed slavery, while the Northern states opposed it. In order to function as a strong nation, the United States government felt that all states must abide by the same laws. The South wished to continue slavery and wanted freedom from central government. Therefore, they decided to secede, or separate, from the United States.

As the Southern states seceded, they took over federal forts. One of these was Fort Sumter, which the Confederates took by force. The firing on United States troops in Fort Sumter started the Civil War. In 1865, the South surrendered and agreed to remain part of the United States. Six hundred thousand soldiers died in the war. Surely, this is why Miss Franny Block tells Opal and Amanda that war should be a curse word.

Activity

Using an encyclopedia or the Internet, answer the questions below.

1. Which Southern states wanted to secede from the nation? _____

    _____

2. Who was president at the time of the Civil War? _____

3. Who was Jefferson Davis, and why was he important to the Civil War? _____

    _____

4. Who was Robert E. Lee, and why was he important to the Civil War? _____

    _____

5. How did Abraham Lincoln die? Who killed him? _____

    _____

Understanding Disabilities

Stevie Dewberry tells Opal that Otis from the pet shop is retarded. Instead of labeling Otis in this way, a more respectful way to talk about his difficulty with thinking is to say that Otis has a developmental disability. People with developmental disabilities may think more slowly. For instance, he kept on playing his guitar after the police told him he wasn't allowed to play music on the street. He may have needed longer than most people to think about their request.

Gloria Dump sees so poorly that Opal decides to read to her. Gloria has a physical disability. A few people are blind from birth. Some people become blind due to complications from disease. Older people may go blind due to deterioration of the eyes, which is most likely what happened to Gloria.

Choose one disability from the list below. Using an encyclopedia or the Internet, answer the questions that follow.

Disability List

- blindness
- deafness
- dyslexia
- Downs syndrome

- autism
- speech impediment
- cerebral palsy
- paralysis

1. Which disability did you choose? _____

2. How does this disability affect a person? _____

3. How does this disability occur? _____

4. What can be done to treat this disability? _____

5. Do you know of anyone who has this disability? If so, what does he or she do to compensate, or make up for, his or her limitations?_____

   _____

6. List three things that you could do to help a person with this particular disability.

   a. _____

   _____

   b. _____

   _____

   c. _____

   _____

Quiz

Answer the following questions about Chapters 16–20.

1. How did the war affect Miss Franny Block's great-grandfather? _____

   _____

2. What causes Opal to be sad as she eats the Littmus Lozenge? _____

   _____

3. How does Opal treat Stevie and Dunlap Dewberry at the end of Chapter 17? _____

   _____

4. Why does Opal's father make her apologize to Stevie Dewberry?_____

   _____

5. What does Opal find out about Amanda's brother Carson? _____

   _____

6. Why did Otis go to jail? _____

   _____

7. Why does Gloria Dump make Opal invite Stevie and Dunlap Dewberry and Amanda Wilkinson to

   the party? _____

   _____

8. How does Opal persuade Otis to come to the party? _____

   _____

Making Candy

Miss Franny Block gives Opal and Amanda Littmus Lozenges—a candy that her great-grandfather manufactured. Opal says, "I ate my Littmus Lozenge slow. It tasted good. It tasted like root beer and strawberry and something else I didn't have a name for, something that made me feel kind of sad."

Fondant—a type of creamy candy—can be flavored any way you like. You might experiment with different flavors, as Miss Franny Block's great-grandfather might have experimented when working on his recipe for Littmus Lozenges.

———————————————— **Basic Fondant** ————————————————

Ingredients

- 2 cups (400 g) sugar
- ⅛ t. (.3 cm) cream of tartar
- flavoring such as vanilla, lemon, root beer, or peppermint extract; cocoa; instant decaffeinated coffee
- food coloring (optional)

Materials

- large, heavy cookie sheet
- dish cloths
- 3-quart (3 litre) heavy pot with cover
- metal spoon
- pastry brush
- candy thermometer
- heavy, metal spatula
- wax paper

Directions

Wipe cookie sheet with a damp cloth. Put the sugar, cream of tartar, and one cup of water in a pot. Stir. Place the pot over medium heat and let mixture come to a boil. Stir until the sugar is completely dissolved. Cover the pot and let the mixture boil for two minutes. Uncover. Dip a pastry brush in cold water and use it to wash down the crystallized sugar on the inside of the pot. Boil without stirring until the syrup reaches 238°F (114°C) on a candy thermometer. Remove the pot from heat and pour the syrup out onto the cookie sheet. Let the syrup cool for ten minutes. Spread candy out with a metal spatula, turning the mixture over and over on itself. As it starts to thicken, add a few drops of flavoring and, if you like, food coloring as you knead the candy by hand. Continue to knead until it is creamy and too stiff to work easily. Cover the candy with a damp cloth and let it stand for 30 minutes. Knead again for one minute. Roll candy into 1" (2.5 cm) balls and set them on a piece of wax paper to dry. Makes 1 pound.

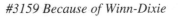

Community Volunteering

Opal loves to read, so she volunteers to read *Gone with the Wind* to Gloria Dump because Gloria can no longer see well.

What particular hobby or talent do you have to share? There are hundreds of ways that you may volunteer in your community to help people less fortunate than you. Retirement homes, local parks, and libraries are always looking for volunteers. For instance, if you are good at math, you may volunteer to tutor a younger student at your school in this subject. If you love animals, you may want to volunteer at your local animal shelter. Someone who is good at playing the piano or guitar may want to give a performance at a hospital or senior center.

Volunteering brings joy to at least two people—the person you're helping and the volunteer. Fill out the first part of the form below. Then, volunteer! After you have offered your help, fill out the second part of the form. Share your experience with the class. (**Note to teacher:** This activity may be completed in school or as homework. Students may need adult assistance to make contact with volunteer coordinators in the community.)

Volunteer Form

Part One

What am I good at doing? _____

Whom would I like to help? _____

Where can I volunteer? _____

With whom do I speak in order to set up a volunteer time? _____

When will I volunteer? _____

Part Two

Where did I volunteer? _____

Whom did I help? _____

Here is a description of my experience: _____

_____

_____

_____

Would I volunteer here again? Why or why not? _____

_____

Thunderstorm!

Winn-Dixie suffers from what Opal's father calls a "pathological fear" of thunderstorms. Unfortunately for Winn-Dixie, there are many thunderstorms in Florida during the summer. A thunderstorm is a storm that produces thunder and lightning. Thunderstorms form when the air close to the ground is warm and humid. When this warm air rises, it cools, and the water vapor in the air condenses, forming a cloud that extends from the ground to the bottom layer of the atmosphere. The greater the temperature difference between the warm cloud and the air surrounding it, the more violent the storm. In temperate areas such as Florida, thunderstorms are more likely to occur in hot summer months than in cooler winter months.

During a thunderstorm, you'll see the lightning before you will hear thunder because light travels faster than sound. Since sound travels at 1,115 feet per second, and there are 5,280 feet in a mile, it will take about four seconds for the sound of thunder to travel one mile.

It is important to stay inside during a thunderstorm. Though it rarely happens, people and animals have been struck and killed by lightning.

The next time you're in a thunderstorm, stay inside and begin to count seconds as soon as you see lightning (one hippopotamus, two hippopotami . . .). See what number you get to when you hear thunder. Remember, for every four seconds, the storm is about a mile away. Continue counting seconds after each flash of lightning to see if the storm is coming closer or moving farther away.

Answer the questions below about thunder and lightning:

1. How many miles away from you is the thunderstorm if you count 12 seconds between the time you see lightning and the time you hear thunder?_____

2. How far away is the storm if you count two seconds between the time you see lightning and the time you hear thunder? _____

3. You hear of a thunderstorm two miles away. How many feet would you have to travel before you were in the middle of the storm?_____

4. Bonus question: Research thunderstorms in an encyclopedia or on the Internet. Then list at least three things you could do in order to stay safe during a thunderstorm.

_____

_____

_____

_____

Life Is Like a Littmus Lozenge

Miss Franny Block's great-grandfather had great success with his Littmus Lozenges. "He manufactured a piece of candy that tasted sweet and sad at the same time," Miss Franny tells Opal. Kate DiCamillo uses Littmus Lozenges as a metaphor for life, which can also be sweet and sad. For example, Opal finds that losing her mother and having to move away from her friends to Naomi are sad events. Later, she rescues Winn-Dixie and makes new friends—both of which add sweetness to her life.

Below, make a list of sweet events and then sad events that have occurred in your life over the years.

Sweet	Sad
1.	1.
2.	2.
3.	3.
4.	4.
5.	5.

Now, make a list of the sweet things that may have come out of the sad things you've experienced in your life. For instance, Opal has to leave her old town and move to Naomi, Florida, where she doesn't know anyone. But then she finds Winn-Dixie and discovers the sweetness of friendship.

1. _____

2. _____

3. _____

4. _____

5. _____

Quiz

Answer the following questions about Chapters 21–26.

1. Why is Opal so glad to see Amanda at the party? _____

_____

2. Why do you think Otis is reluctant to go to the party?_____

_____

3. What does Opal's father mean when he says, "We appreciate the complicated and wonderful gifts you give us in each other"? _____

_____

4. Why does Opal forget about Winn-Dixie? _____

_____

5. What does Gloria say to Opal about loving something?_____

_____

6. Why does Opal's father cry? _____

_____

7. How do Opal's friends find Winn-Dixie? _____

_____

8. How does Dunlap surprise Opal at the end of the book? _____

_____

Luminarias

Before the party, Opal and Gloria Dump fill up paper bags with sand and then put candles inside them. They put the bags all around the yard and then light the candles. These party decorations are called *luminarias*. People in Mexico and other cultures use these lanterns during traditional Christmas celebrations.

Materials

- one paper lunch bag per student

- small scoop of sand per student

- one votive candle per student

- scissors

- matches (for teacher use only)

Directions

(**Note to teacher:** Supervise students at all times when matches are used and candles are lit.)

Using scissors, cut out several small shapes such as diamonds, circles, or squares in your paper bag. (The candlelight will shine through these shapes at night and cast them on the ground.)

Place sand in the paper bag. Scoop out a hollow in the center of the sand, and place the candle in the hollow. Make sure that the candle is securely placed in the sand.

Arrange the luminarias in a pattern or use them to line a walkway. Light the candles and enjoy!

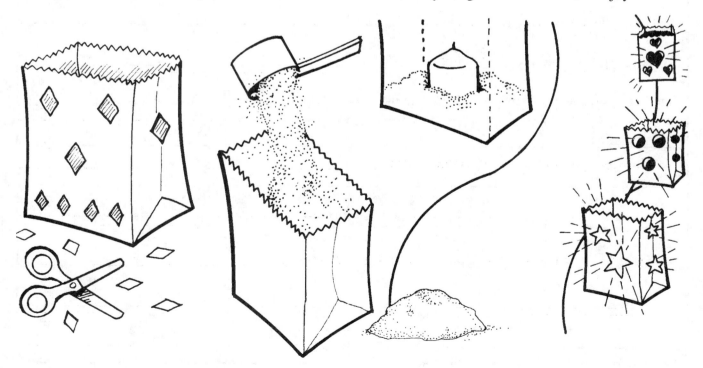

Classmate Interviews

Opal learns a great deal about people during the course of this novel. She learns that Otis is not a criminal, and that Gloria Dump is not a witch but is instead a wonderful woman. She finds out that Amanda is sad because her little brother drowned. She even finds out that Stevie and Dunlap Dewberry aren't "bald-headed babies" but are actually nice boys who just want to be her friend. Soon, she will be able to list ten things about each of her new friends, just as she's able to do about her mother and Winn-Dixie.

Choose a classmate whom you do not know well. Using the form below, interview this classmate. Then let your classmate interview you. Finally, introduce your new friend to the rest of the class by reading your form aloud.

What is your first, middle, and last name? _____

When is your birthday? _____

Where were you born?_____

What is your favorite animal? _____

What is your favorite food? _____

What is your favorite thing to do?_____

Where do you like to spend time?_____

What is your favorite subject in school? _____

What do you want to be when you grow up? _____

Think of your own question to ask. Write it here and then record your classmate's answer.

_____

_____

_____

_____

_____

Egg Salad Sandwiches and Dump Punch

Opal and Gloria Dump make egg salad sandwiches for their party. "We cut them up in triangles and cut off the crusts and put little toothpicks with frilly tops in them." Even Winn-Dixie gets an egg salad sandwich!

——— Egg Salad Sandwiches ———

Ingredients

- two loaves of bread
- two dozen hard-boiled eggs
- 1 cup (236 mL) mayonnaise
- salt and pepper
- curry powder (optional)
- pickle relish (optional)

Materials

- wooden spoon
- large bowl
- sharp knife
- cutting board
- frilly toothpicks
- plate

Directions

(**Note to teacher:** Supervise students when handling knives.) Peel the eggs and mash them in a bowl with the mayonnaise. Leave them lumpy or mash them smooth, depending upon your preference. Season the salad with salt and pepper. You may also choose to season your egg salad with two or three tablespoons of curry powder or pickle relish. Spread the mixture onto 16 pieces of bread. Place another slice of bread on top of each sandwich. Slice each sandwich diagonally into four triangles. Put a toothpick through each triangle and arrange sandwiches on a plate. Recipe makes 48 small sandwiches.

——— Dump Punch ———

Gloria says that she is world famous for a drink she calls Dump Punch. Here is a recipe she might use.

Ingredients

- one quart or liter of each: orange juice, grapefruit juice, lemon-lime soda

Materials

- large bowl
- long-handled spoon
- ladle
- cups

Directions

Dump the liquids into a bowl, stir, and serve! Recipe makes three quarts or liters.

Making Friends

Opal learns a great deal about friendship in *Because of Winn-Dixie*. Over the summer, she finds that anyone can be friends—no matter what their age or species. List the friends Opal makes on the lines below:

_____

_____

_____

During an interview about her novel, Kate DiCamillo said that friends have been "the saving grace" in her life. Her friends, like Opal's, are valuable. Think about the qualities that make a good friend and list them:

_____

_____

_____

Think about one of your best friends. What makes this person such a good friend? Record this person's good qualities in the space below.

_____

_____

_____

Good friends are generous. They help each other out and listen to each other's troubles. Gloria Dump listens to Opal. Opal reads to Gloria Dump. Opal and Amanda listen to Miss Franny Block's stories. Later, she gives them Littmus Lozenges. What can you do to be a good friend? List three ideas:

1. _____

2. _____

3. _____

Opal did not think that Amanda, Sweetie Pie, or Stevie and Dunlap Dewberry would become her friends, but they do. Think of someone with whom you would like to be friends. What might you do in order to become friends with this person?

_____

_____

_____

Any Questions?

When you finished reading *Because of Winn-Dixie*, did you have questions that were left unanswered? Write some of your questions here.

_____

_____

_____

Work in groups or by yourself to predict possible answers for some or all of the questions you have asked above, as well as those written below. When you have finished, share your predictions with your class.

- Does Opal's mother come back? _____

- Does Winn-Dixie run away again? _____

- Does Opal get another dog to keep Winn-Dixie company? _____

- Do Opal and Amanda become best friends? _____

- Does Otis play his guitar for people again? If so, for whom? _____

- How does Opal like her new school? _____

- What happens to Winn-Dixie while Opal is at school? _____

- Does the preacher find himself a new wife and Opal a new mother? _____

- Do other people volunteer to read to Gloria Dump? If so, who? _____

- Does Sweetie Pie finally get a pet? If so, what kind? _____

- Do Dunlap and Opal become good friends? _____

- What kind of job does Opal have when she grows up? _____

- Does Miss Franny Block ever see her bear again? _____

- Does Opal finally meet Gertrude, the owner of the pet store? _____

- Do Stevie and Dunlap become friends with Gloria Dump? _____

- Who comes to Sweetie Pie's birthday party? _____

- Does Amanda ever get another little brother? _____

Book Report Ideas

There are several ways to report on a book after you have read it. When you have finished *Because of Winn-Dixie*, choose a method of reporting from the list below, or come up with your own idea on how best to report on this book.

Make a Book Jacket

Design a book jacket for this book. On the front, draw a picture that you feel captures the story. On the back, write a paragraph or two that summarizes the main points of the book.

Make a Time Line

On paper, create a time line to show the significant events in Opal's life the summer she moves to Naomi. You may illustrate your time line, if you wish.

Design a Scrapbook

Use magazine pictures, photographs, and other illustrations to create a scrapbook that Opal might keep to document her first summer in Naomi. She might choose to decorate her scrapbook with stickers, or to include a letter to her mother. She might also include pictures of her new friends and one of her father's sermons.

Make a Collage

Using old magazines and photographs, design a collage that illustrates all of Opal's adventures in *Because of Winn-Dixie*.

Create a Time Capsule

What items might Opal put in a time capsule by which to remember her summer? What container might she use as a time capsule?

Write a Biography

Do research to find out about the life of Kate DiCamillo. You may use the Internet (Candlewick Press has a Web site about this author at *www.candlewick.com)* or magazines. Write a biography showing how Kate DiCamillo's experiences might have influenced her novel.

Act Out a Play

With one or two other students, write a play featuring some of the characters in this novel. Then act out your play for your class.

Design a Diorama

Using a shoebox as a frame, create a diorama that illustrates an important scene in the novel. You may use all sorts of materials (paper, sand, clay, paint, fabric, etc.) to bring this scene to life.

Make Puppets

Using a variety of materials, design puppets to represent one or all of the characters in this novel. You may decide to work with other students to write and perform a puppet show.

Research Ideas

As you read *Because of Winn-Dixie*, you discovered geographical locations, events, and people about which you might wish to know more. To increase your understanding of the characters, places, and events in this novel, do research to find additional information.

Work alone or in groups to find out more about one or more of the items listed below. You may use books, magazines, and the Internet to do your research. Afterwards, share your findings with the class.

- Florida
- single parents
- stray dogs
- Baptist church
- alcoholism
- constellations
- history of your public library
- parrots
- planting a tree
- thunderstorms
- animal charmers
- *Gone With the Wind*
- Civil War
- Fort Sumter

- luminarias
- Southern dialect
- running
- guitars
- street performers
- developmental disabilities
- mental health
- Newbery Award
- prejudice
- volunteer opportunities for children
- gardening
- divorce
- animal rights organizations
- Gainesville

Party Time!

Planning the Party

Opal discovers that a party is a wonderful way to bring good people together. She and Gloria have fun planning, preparing, and hosting a party. Each of Opal's friends brings something unique to the party to help make it festive.

Your class will enjoy planning, preparing for, and participating in its own party.

Party Checklist

Three weeks before the party . . .

❏ decide when and where the party will occur.

❏ think of a theme for the party. Themes related to this book include dogs, books, and Florida. Your class may opt for non-book related themes such as a holiday party, or one to celebrate a season or school-related event.

❏ decide whether your class wants to invite guests to the party. If so, make and send the invitations on page 39.

❏ discuss decorations. Will you use crepe paper, luminarias, and magazine pictures, like Opal and her friends; or will you use something entirely different to make your party look festive?

Two weeks before the party . . .

❏ decide what food and/or drink you will make as a class. This book provides recipes for egg salad sandwiches, Dump Punch, and candy. Make a grocery list.

❏ pass around a sign-up sheet. Each student should be encouraged to bring something unique to the party. They might bring food, sign up to play musical instruments, bring a favorite (small) pet, or show off a skill (such as juggling or gymnastics).

❏ send home a note to students' parents to let them know the date and time of the party, as well as what the student signed up to bring.

One week before the party . . .

❏ send home a note reminding students of what they are to bring for the party.

❏ buy and/or make decorations.

The day before the party . . .

❏ make egg salad and candy.

The day of the party . . .

❏ decorate the party space.

❏ finish making egg salad sandwiches.

❏ make Dump Punch.

Party Time *(cont.)*

Come to a Party!

Day: _____

Time: _____

Place: _____

Hosts: _____

Theme: _____

Dog Songs

Opal and her friends sing songs at their party. Talk to your school's music teacher and ask if he/she might locate and teach your class songs relating to dogs. Here are some to get you started.

Bingo

There was a farmer who

Had a dog,

And Bingo was his name—oh!

B-I-N-G-O!

B-I-N-G-O!

B-I-N-G-O!

And Bingo was his name—oh!

There was a farmer

Had a dog,

And Bingo was his name—oh!

(Students clap)-I-N-G-O!

(Clap)-I-N-G-O!

(Clap)-I-N-G-O!

And Bingo was his name—oh!

Continue the song, clapping in place of "B" and "I" in the third verse, then in place of "B," "I," and "N" in the fourth verse, and so on.

E-I, E-I, Oh

Old MacDonald had a farm.

E-I, E-I, oh!

And on this farm he had a dog.

E-I, E-I, oh!

With a "Woof! Woof!" here,

And a "Woof! Woof!" there.

Here a "Woof!"

There a "Woof!"

Everywhere a "Woof! Woof!"

Old MacDonald had a farm.

E-I, E-I, oh!

(Substitute any animal/bird in place of "dog,"
Students will love mimicking the various animal/bird

Games

Perhaps, after the thunderstorm cleared, Opal and her friends went out to Gloria Dump's yard and played games. Here are some games they might have played.

Relay Races

Divide students into three or four teams. Explain that in order for teams to be strong, they need to support and cheer on every member. Form the teams into lines behind a starting line. Choose a turnaround point and explain that the first team member will run to that point, then turn around and run back, touching the hand of the next team member, who then runs.

There are numerous fun variations on the running relay race. You might ask students to do the following:

- run on all fours while barking like dogs
- walk like ducks
- skip
- hop
- jump
- somersault
- walk balancing a book on one's head

Steal the Dog Bone

Divide the class in two. On the playground, line each team up horizontally on two lines, 50 feet apart. Draw a circle three feet in diameter directly between the two lines. Place a chalkboard eraser in the middle of the circle.

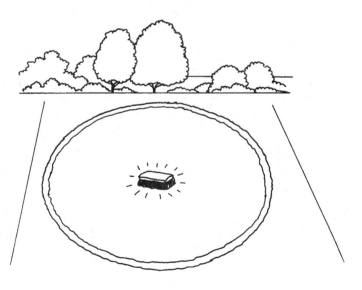

Assign each student on one team a number (for instance, between 1 and 15). Then assign each student on the other team identical numbers, so that there are two "number ones," two "number twos," and so on. Explain that you will call out a number, and the person from each team who has that number must run toward the circle and try to "steal" the dog bone (eraser). The student should try to make it back with the bone to his or her original spot in the line up without being tagged by the student from the opposing team member. This earns one point. If the student is tagged by the other team member while holding the bone, the other team gets a point.

Make sure to call all numbers at least once so that every student gets a turn to play.

Field Trips and Class Visits

Now that your students have learned about dogs, they may enjoy taking one or more field trips to canine service agencies or having someone who works with dogs visit the class. Choose an activity from the list below and locate the appropriate person in the phone book. Be sure to call at least two weeks in advance to give the staff plenty of time to prepare for your students' visit.

The Humane Society (or local shelter): Volunteers lead tours of the facility, as well as discuss responsible pet ownership. Some branches will send volunteers directly to your classroom with dogs and/or cats.

Dog Trainers: Local trainers may be pleased to give your class a demonstration of their work, either with live dogs or on videotape. If permitted by your administrators, encourage the trainer to leave behind information for students to share with parents.

Dog Groomers: Local groomers can bring a dog into the classroom to demonstrate the fine points of dog grooming. They may also be able to talk about grooming for dog shows. As in "Dog Trainers" (above), groomers may be able to leave behind information.

Pet Stores: You may opt to visit a local pet store in order to look at dogs. Discuss with students their feelings about the puppies in cages. Tell them about dog breeding and lead a discussion about buying a purebred dog versus rescuing one from a shelter.

Dog Shows: Your city may sponsor a local dog show. If so, see if you can get a discounted attendance rate. Students may be able to interview participants and watch various competitions.

Hold a Dog Show: With parents' assistance, hold a dog show or dog parade on a weekday afternoon or a Saturday. Give each dog a personalized prize-ribbon (Best Floppy Ears, Fluffiest Tail, etc.). You could also hold a similar show with stuffed toy dogs in the classroom.

Dog Parks: Most cities have an off-leash area in which dogs can run. Find your city's local dog park by calling the parks and recreation office or looking on the Web site *www.dogpark.com*. Students may visit the dog park to observe how dogs socialize with each other, as well as how owners work with dogs on obedience.

Dog Kennels: Where can you take your dogs when you go on vacation? Many kennels will be happy to give students a tour of their facilities. They may invite students to visit their recreational areas and grooming areas, as well as answer questions about homesickness and the importance of vaccinations.

Dog Rescue: Most dog breeds have a group of people who will place dogs who need new homes with carefully chosen owners. Greyhounds, in particular, have many groups that rescue and place them. Call your local animal shelter to find out about these rescue groups.

Objective Test and Essay

Matching: Match the descriptions of each character with their names.

_____	1.	India Opal Buloni	**a.** takes Opal's hand to help her up, and races with her
_____	2.	the preacher	**b.** writes sermons and feels sad because his wife is gone
_____	3.	Winn-Dixie	**c.** runs the library in Naomi and tells wonderful stories
_____	4.	Miss Franny Block	**d.** likes to tease Opal about witches
_____	5.	Amanda Wilkinson	**e.** found in a grocery store; he is terrified of thunderstorms
_____	6.	Sweetie Pie Thomas	**f.** moved to Naomi at age ten and rescued a dog
_____	7.	Otis	**g.** works in a pet store and plays the guitar
_____	8.	Stevie Dewberry	**h.** hosts a party for Opal's friends and makes punch
_____	9.	Dunlap Dewberry	**i.** she's sad because she lost her little brother
_____	10.	Gloria Dump	**j.** wants a pet and is about to turn six years old

True or False: Answer true or false in the blanks below.

1. _____ Opal brought Winn-Dixie to Naomi with her when she moved.

2. _____ Opal has several friends who are adults.

3. _____ The preacher tells Opal all about her mother without being asked.

4. _____ Gloria Dump is really a witch.

5. _____ Opal gets all her friends together in one place for a party.

Short Answer: Write a brief response on separate paper.

1. Why did Opal's mother leave her?

2. Why does Opal decide to take Winn-Dixie home?

3. List the friends that Opal makes during her first summer in Naomi.

4. What does Opal realize during her conversation with her father after Winn-Dixie is lost?

Essay: Respond to the following on separate paper.

Opal finds happiness when she stops thinking about her own problems and starts thinking about how to help others. Among the people she helps are Gloria Dump, Otis, and Amanda Wilkinson. She also helps Winn-Dixie. Explain what Opal does to help each of these characters. Then explain how they help her.

Responding to Quotes

On separate paper, respond to the following quotes as selected by your instructor.

Chapter One: "'Wait a minute!' I hollered. 'That's my dog. Don't call the pound.'"

Chapter Two: "Sometimes he reminded me of a turtle hiding inside its shell, in there thinking about things, and not ever sticking his head out into the world."

Chapter Three: "'I've been talking to him and he agreed with me that, since I'm ten years old, you should tell me ten things about my mama.'"

Chapter Four: "'She drank. She drank beer. And whiskey. And wine. Sometimes, she couldn't stop drinking. And that made me and your mama fight quite a bit.'"

Chapter Five: "And everybody started laughing and clapping. The preacher picked up the mouse by the tail and walked and threw it out the front door of the Pick-It-Quick, and everybody applauded again."

Chapter Eleven: "'Opal, I believe Winn-Dixie has a pathological fear of thunderstorms.'"

Chapter Twelve: "'I take them out. I feel sorry for them being locked up all the time. I know what it's like, being locked up.'"

Chapter Thirteen: "'My mama says you shouldn't be spending all your time cooped up in that pet shop and at that library, sitting around talking with old ladies. She says you should get out in the fresh air and play with kids your own age.'"

Chapter Fourteen: "'…you can't always judge people by the things they done. You got to judge them by what they are doing now.'"

Chapter Sixteen: "'War,' said Miss Franny with her eyes still closed, 'should be a cuss word, too.'"

Chapter Nineteen: "I thought about my mama. Thinking about her was the same as the hole you keep on feeling with your tongue after you lose a tooth. Time after time, my mind kept going to that empty spot, the spot where I felt like she should be."

Chapter Twenty-three: "'There ain't no way you can hold on to something that wants to go, you understand? You can only love what you got while you got it.'"

Chapter Twenty-four: "'You always give up!' I shouted. 'You're always pulling your head inside your stupid old turtle shell. I bet you didn't even go out looking for my mama when she left.'"

Chapter Twenty-six: "'Let's sing,' said Sweetie Pie, opening her eyes and sitting up straight. 'Let's sing for the dog.'"

Conversations

Work in groups according to the numbers in parentheses to write or act out the conversations that might have occurred in each of the following situations in *Because of Winn-Dixie*.

- Opal and her father deal with Winn-Dixie on the first day of school. *(2 people)*

- Opal and Amanda decide to be best friends. *(2 people)*

- Opal and Amanda go to Sweetie Pie's sixth birthday party. *(3 people)*

- Sweetie Pie persuades her mother to get her a dog like Winn-Dixie. *(2 people)*

- Miss Franny Block asks Otis to play guitar at the library. *(2 people)*

- Amanda tells Opal about her brother's drowning. *(2 people)*

- Gloria Dump shows Opal's father the bottle tree in her backyard. *(2 people)*

- Opal's mother comes home to see Opal and her father. *(3 people)*

- Miss Franny Block's bear returns to Naomi, and Otis charms it with his guitar. *(2 people)*

- Stevie and Dunlap volunteer to read books to Gloria Dump. *(3 people)*

- Another thunderstorm happens while Opal is in school, and she has to persuade the teacher to let her go find her dog. *(2 people)*

- Miss Franny Block, Gloria Dump, and Otis plan Opal's eleventh birthday party. *(3 people)*

- Opal and Dunlap become friends and start a dog-walking service. *(2 people)*

- Two hunters walk into the library with the book Miss Franny Block lost to the bear years ago, and ask her if she recognizes it. *(3 people)*

- Opal brings home a stray cat, and she and her father talk about whether Winn-Dixie can live with it. *(2 people)*

- Otis tells Opal what really happened the day he was locked in jail. *(2 people)*

- Miss Franny Block tells Sweetie Pie about the Civil War and the meaning of prejudice. *(2 people)*

Bibliography of Related Reading

Fiction

Armstrong, William Howard. *Sounder*. HarperTrade, 2001.

Estes, Eleanor. *Ginger Pye*. HarperTrade, 2000.

Fleischman, Sid. *Jim Ugly*. Turtleback, 1992.

Gipson, Fred. *Old Yeller*. HarperTrade, 2001.

Jocelyn, Marthe. *The Invisible Harry*. Tundra, 1999.

Kjelgaard, Jim. *Big Red*. Turtleback, 1976.

Knight, Eric Mowbray. *Lassie Come Home*. Harmony Rain, 1981.

London, Jack. *Call of the Wild*. Meadowbrook Press, 1999.

Naylor, Phyllis Reynolds. *Shiloh*. Atheneum, 1991.

Rawls, Wilson. *Where the Red Fern Grows*. Turtleback, 1996.

Tamar, Erika. *The Junkyard Dog*. Turtleback, 1997.

Taylor, Theodore. *The Trouble with Tuck*. Turtleback, 2000.

Terhune, Albert Payson. *Lad: A Dog*. Puffin, 1993.

Van de Velde, Vivian. *Smart Dog*. Harcourt, 1998.

Wallace, Bill. *A Dog Called Kitty*. Holiday House, 1980.

Nonfiction

Karwoski, Gail. *Seaman: The Dog Who Explored the West with Lewis & Clark*. Peachtree, 1999.

Rosenthal, Lisa. *A Dog's Best Friend: An Activity Book for Kids and Their Dogs*. Chicago Review Press, 1999.

Singer, Marilyn. *A Dog's Gotta Do what a Dog's Gotta Do: Dogs at Work*. Henry Holt, 2000.

Web Site

http://encarta.msn.com/ (Type in the search term *dogs*.)

Answer Key

Page 10

1. Opal rescues Winn-Dixie by telling the grocery store manager that he is her dog.

2. Opal likes the fact that Winn-Dixie looks like he's smiling and that he, like her, doesn't have a family.

3. Opal feels that her father spends too much time working. She's frustrated that he seldom communicates with her.

4. Opal's father agrees to let her keep Winn-Dixie because the dog puts his head in the preacher's lap.

5. Opal washes Winn-Dixie with baby shampoo and tries to brush his teeth.

6. Opal's mother left her and the preacher because she was an alcoholic who was tired of being a preacher's wife.

7. The preacher allows Winn-Dixie to go to church because he feels sorry for him, and because the dog protests so loudly about staying home alone.

8. Opal prays that she may tell the story of Winn-Dixie to her mother. She also prays to make friends, and for the mouse that her dog has caught.

Page 15

1. Miss Franny Block allows Winn-Dixie into the library because he walks in and lies down at her feet.

2. When she was a little girl, Miss Franny asked her father to give her a library for her birthday.

3. Opal promises to help Otis clean the pet store so that she can earn Winn-Dixie a collar and leash.

4. Opal is happy at the end of Chapter 8 because she has finally made a friend, gotten a job, and been invited to a birthday party.

5. Opal doesn't like Stevie and Dunlap because they tease her and call Gloria Dump a witch.

6. Opal goes into Gloria's yard to find Winn-Dixie.

7. Winn-Dixie scares Miss Franny so that she tells Opal a story about a bear. He needs a leash and collar, so Opal befriends Otis. Sweetie Pie likes him, which makes her talk to Opal. Then he runs into Gloria's yard, and they become friends.

8. Opal is amazed at the end of Chapter 10 that her father allows Winn-Dixie on the bed and laughs.

Page 18

Population—approximately 15,000,000 people

Area—59,988 square miles (155,368 square kilometers)

Capital City—Tallahassee

State Flower—Orange Blossom

State Motto—"In God We Trust"

State Bird—Mockingbird

State Nickname—The Sunshine State

Time Zone—Eastern

Climate—Humid, subtropical

National Park(s)—Everglades; Gulf Islands; Big Cypress

1. Gainesville is closest to the Atlantic Ocean.

2. The three largest cities in Florida are Jacksonville, Miami, and Tampa.

3. A peninsula is a finger of land jutting out into water.

4. Cuba is directly south of Florida.

5. South America is southwest of Florida.

Page 20

1. Opal's father says that Winn-Dixie has a pathological fear of thunderstorms because the dog races around the house terrified.

2. Opal feels love for her father because he obviously cares for Winn-Dixie.

3. Otis plays music for the animals in the pet shop because he feels sorry for them being caged.

4. Opal and Winn-Dixie go to Gertrude's Pets, then to the library, and finally to Gloria Dump's house.

5. Opal gets mad at Stevie because he says his mother said Opal should not be hanging around with old people. He also calls Otis "retarded."

6. Gloria Dump has a bottle tree in her yard to remind her of her past alcoholism.

7. Gloria tells Opal to judge people by what they're like now.

8. Opal holds tightly onto Winn-Dixie because she doesn't want to lose him the way she lost her mother, and because she loves him.

Answer Key *(cont.)*

Page 23

1. South Carolina, Mississippi, Florida, Alabama, Georgia, Louisiana, Texas, Virginia, Arkansas, North Carolina, Tennessee.

2. Abraham Lincoln

3. Jefferson Davis was the president of the Confederate States of America. He was important because he supported the secession.

4. Lee was the general of the Confederate Army who eventually surrendered to Ulysses S. Grant.

5. Abraham Lincoln was assassinated by John Wilkes Booth.

Page 25

1. Miss Franny's great-grandfather went to war as a child. He was hungry, cold, hot, itchy, and shot at. When he returned home, he found his home burned and his family dead. He cried, and then he built a candy factory.

2. Opal is sad because she misses her mother, because she had to leave all her friends, and because Stevie and Dunlap tease her.

3. Opal waves at Stevie and Dunlap.

4. Opal's father makes her apologize to Stevie because he says Stevie is just trying to be Opal's friend.

5. Opal finds out that Amanda's brother drowned.

6. Otis went to jail because he played his guitar on the street and wouldn't stop when the police told him to.

7. Gloria makes Opal invite Stevie, Dunlap, and Amanda to the party because they're Opal's age and she wants Opal to get to know them.

8. Opal persuades Otis to come to the party by promising to clean up the pet shop for a whole week free of charge.

Page 30

1. Opal is glad to see Amanda at the party because she feels sorry for her after she finds out her brother drowned.

2. Otis may be reluctant to go to the party because he is shy or unsure of how to act around a group of people he doesn't know.

3. Opal's father means that people, in spite of their complications, are wonderful and generous.

4. Opal forgets about Winn-Dixie because she's busy saving the sandwiches and helping Gloria Dump.

5. Gloria says that you can only love something while you have it.

6. Opal's father cries in sorrow over the loss of his wife.

7. They find Winn-Dixie under a bed. They hear him sneezing.

8. Dunlap surprises Opal by taking her hand to help her up.

Page 43

Matching

1. f		6. j	
2. b		7. g	
3. e		8. d	
4. c		9. a	
5. i		10. h	

True or False

1. False		4. False	
2. True		5. True	
3. False			

Short Answer

1. Opal's mother left her because she was an alcoholic and didn't like being the wife of a preacher.

2. Opal decides to take Winn-Dixie home because he is obviously a stray, and the store manager is about to call the pound. Her father says she should try to help those less fortunate than she.

3. During her first summer in Naomi, Opal makes the following friends: Miss Franny Block, Otis, Gloria Dump, Amanda Wilkinson, Sweetie Pie Thomas, Dunlap and Stevie Dewberry, and Winn-Dixie.

4. Opal realizes her mother isn't coming back, and that her father feels horrible about this.

Essay

Answers will vary. Accept reasonable and well-supported answers.

Page 44

Grade students on their comprehension of the story as evidenced by the lengths of answers and depths of responses.

Page 45

Grade students on comprehension of the story, knowledge of the characters, and creativity.